LEGENDS FROM MEXICO & CENTRAL AME.

A TEACHER'S GUIDE TO

A QUETZALCÓATL

Tale of The Ball Game

by Marilyn Parke and Sharon Panik

Consultants to the Series
R. Robert and Maria Elena Robbins

Fearon Teacher Aids
Simon & Schuster Supplementary Education Group

About the Authors

Marilyn Parke is a reading specialist with a Master's degree and has been teaching in the elementary grades for over twenty years. She and her husband live in Colorado and have four children.

Sharon Panik is an elementary teacher specializing in reading and learning disabilities, has a Master's degree, and has been teaching for eighteen years. She and her husband live in Colorado and have one child.

Lynn Castle has her B.F.A. in Art History and is currently the curator of the Art Museum of Southeast Texas in Beaumont. She is married and has one child.

Editorial Director: Virginia L. Murphy
Editors: Virginia Massey Bell and Lisa Schwimmer
Cover Illustration: Lynn Castle
Inside Illustration: Teena Remer
Cover and Inside Design: Marek/Janci Design

ISBN 0-86653-960-3

Printed in the United States of America
1.9 8 7 6 5 4 3 2

Contents

Introduction

Understanding and appreciating other cultures is an important educational goal. Mexico is our closest southern neighbor and many students in the United States have Mexican roots. This teacher's guide, along with the book *A Quetzalcóatl Tale of The Ball Game,* provides anthropological, literary, and historical information about pre-Columbian Mexico. A Spanish translation of the ball game story is also available and appropriate for ESL, bilingual, and secondary language classes.

For centuries, stories of the god, Quetzalcóatl, have been part of the ancient Maya, Aztec, and Mexican cultures of Mesoamerica, the region that includes Mexico and Central America. These Quetzalcóatl tales are ancient legends that provide a wonderful ethnic-based reading experience for all children. The legend of the ball game is one of a series of Mesoamerican tales that provides elementary students with an interdisciplinary approach to literature, reading, social studies, drama, music, and art.

Synopsis of The Ball Game Story

Two gods—Tlaloc, the often violent rain god, and Quetzalcóatl, a kind and gentle feathered serpent—want to determine who is the mightiest of all gods. Instead of a war, which would hurt the people of the earth, Quetzalcóatl suggests they play a game with a rubber ball. The winner of the game will be declared the mightiest of all gods. Tlaloc agrees and a huge stone ball court is built by the people of the earth. The two gods establish the rules of the game and begin a long and difficult match. In the end, Quetzalcóatl wins. Tlaloc offers his most precious gift—maize (corn)—as the prize. But Quetzalcóatl doesn't want Tlaloc's people to go hungry, so he chooses jade and quetzal feathers as his prize instead. A surprised Tlaloc quickly grants what he considers Quetzalcóatl's foolish wish and happily keeps the maize for himself and his people.

Background Information

The Maya

Although the culture of the ancient Maya reached its highest levels of achievement between 200 A.D. and 900 A.D., the Mayan Indians have lived in southern Mexico and Central America continuously since before the time of Christ.

The culture of the Maya has always been based in farming and trading. The clothing the Maya wore was made expressly for the hot climate—the women wore light, cloth skirts made from cotton and other fibers and the men wore cotton loincloths. Their homes were built for the climate as well. Houses were made from long poles tied together and the roofs were thatched with grass and palm leaves.

The ancient Maya were very religious, worshipping many gods. Many of the gods were tied in one way or another to agriculture. Religion played a large role in the Mayan culture, with each day of the year having some religious significance. They had ceremonies, festivals, rituals, and celebrations, all based on their many gods—gods of rain, corn, sun, moon, medicine, weaving, and so on. Masks were used by Mesoamerican priests in ceremonial services to depict the various gods whom they represented. Frequently, Quetzalcóatl was shown wearing a white or red mask. Tlaloc often wore a blue mask. Other gods were depicted in other colors. Different Mesoamerican groups described these same gods in various ways, according to their own unique traditions.

Corn was one of the most important aspects of Mesoamerican culture. A farmer working two months could feed a family of six for an entire year, supplementing their diet with vegetables, beans, meat, and spices. Thus, there was leisure time that could be given to the arts, sciences, and public constructions.

During their time of greatest achievement, the Maya built one of the most advanced civilizations on earth, on a par with Egypt, China, Babylon, Rome, and Greece. The Maya were one of the few cultures on earth that developed their own mathematics and writing systems. Some of the most magnificent art in the world was created by the Maya. Their ceremonial centers included pyramids and plazas and rivaled the structures built in other major societies.

The Maya made spectacular achievements in astronomy and constructed complex calendars based on the motion of the sun, moon, stars, and planets. Many of their discoveries were not surpassed in accuracy until the 19th century.

For reasons that have never been discovered, the southern Maya, in cities of the southern highlands centered in Guatemala, declined from their high levels of achievement. The ruling elite and nobility of the Maya disappeared. The people in these areas settled back into the less complicated society that we see there today. The northern Maya, up into the Yucatan, continued to prosper and grow, almost into the 1300s.

The Aztec

The origin of the Aztec Indians is not well-documented, but they came from the north to settle in the heart of the central Mexican valley in the 1300s. At first, their major resource was farming, but by 1500 A.D., they controlled much of central and southern Mexico and constructed an empire built on conquest and tribute.

The men wore loincloths and cloaks and the women and girls wore loose, light blouses and wrap-around skirts. They had homes designed for the climate—houses of adobe in the hot highlands and homes of reeds or branches with thatched roofs in the cooler lowlands.

Their main food source was corn, like the Maya. They made tlaxcallis, which we know as tortillas. They ate these flat corn cakes with vegetables and meat.

Religion was also a very prominent part of the life of the Aztec people, and they, too, had many gods, including gods of agriculture. Their holidays and celebrations were based on their religious beliefs—they had celebrations and ceremonies for the gods of rain, sun, corn, spring and regrowth, fire, and so on. Like the Maya, Aztec priests used masks to depict the gods in their ceremonies.

The Aztec culture was relatively short-lived. They did not surpass the Mayan accomplishments in writing, astronomy, and other learned areas. But they built monumental cities and were similar to the Romans—good warriors, road builders, and engineers. They created a magnificent empire in less than 200 years—the capital city of Tenochtitlán was described by lieutenants of Cortes during the Spanish Entrada as even more grand than anything they had seen in Spain and the Old World.

Life in Mexico and Central America Today

The people of Mexico and Central America today live in cities, towns, and villages, much like the people of the United States. The chief food staple of the Mexicans and Central Americans is still corn. Tortillas are thin, flat cakes made from corn flour that are eaten like bread. Tortillas and corn flour are used to make many dishes, such as tacos, fried tortillas filled with meat or cheese; tostadas, fried tortillas served with vegetables and beans, with cheese on top; and tamales, corn flour dough filled with meat and steamed. Many of these foods are eaten in the United States as well.

There are some 5 million Maya living today in Mexico, Guatemala, Honduras, and Belize. Anthropologists are learning that the Maya have carried forward an unexpectedly rich lore of traditions, mythology, and astronomical knowledge. Thus, the Maya have retained a cultural identity and unity to this very day.

There is a very large population of Mexican Americans in the United States. Mexico is the United States' closest neighbor. Much of the southwestern United States is steeped in Mexican culture.

The Ball Game

The ball game has an ancient history. Mesoamerican scholars think that the ball game probably originated in the lowlands of the Gulf of Mexico and may have been invented as long ago as 1250 B.C. Evidence of ball courts have been found from central Arizona to Honduras and have also included some of the Caribbean islands.

The ball game became a universal ritual throughout many ages and cultures. The game was played as pure sport, as a vehicle for wagers and ceremonies, and as a means of settling differences as well. As the ball game was assimilated into different cultures, the significance, rules, and form of the game changed over the many centuries.

The Mesoamerican ball courts evolved differently according to the cultures represented. In almost every major Meso-american archaeological site, there is at least one ball court, often there are many. One of the ball courts discovered was even larger than a modern-day football field. On either side of some of these ball courts were two stone walls with a temple at each end and platforms for spectators. In the center of each wall was a large stone ring that allowed a ball to pass through with just a finger width to spare.

Area where the ball game was originally played.

Some ball courts had no rings at all and used goal markers. The rules of the game varied with the different cultures.

In the beginning, the game was played with a hard rubber ball that was thrown by hand. Later, players probably used bats.

An Aztec rendering of a ball court.

Eventually the ballplayers were not allowed to use their hands at all. They struck the ball with their hips, knees, and elbows which were padded with cotton and leather.

Two teams with up to six members on each team faced each other from diagonal corners of the court. The captain or leader threw the ball into the middle of the courtyard to start the game. The object of the game was to pass the ball to other members of the team and stop the opposition from getting the ball. A point was scored against the opposing team every time the ball was put into play on the opponent's side.

It was extremely difficult to pass the hard, six-inch diameter ball through the small stone hoop. When this did occur, the game was immediately over and the team accomplishing this feat won the game, no matter how many points the opponents had previously scored. Sometimes the game continued for several days until a winner was declared.

Often the games were played just for fun. It was common for great wagers to be made. Wealthy lords brought gold, jade, and fine clothing to bet. After the game, the victors were given large rewards and sometimes had the opportunity to acquire the clothing and possessions of the spectators—if they could chase and catch them!

The game may also have been played at more serious levels. The ball court itself was a temple. Omens may have been read into the behavior and movement of the ball from each of the four quarters of the court.

The alignment of the ball courts may have had an astronomical significance.

If a ball court extended north and south, it may have symbolized the sun's seasonal motions from north to south throughout the year. If a ball court were aligned east to west, this may have represented the sun's daily journey across the sky, through the underworld, and then its rebirth the next morning.

Confrontation between enemies often took place on the ball court as well. Opponents regularly turned to the ball game to resolve conflicts. The settlement of differences between groups is a major concept that can be learned from the story of the Mesoamerican ball game.

The symbolism of the Mesoamerican ball game is still open for different interpretations. The story that the authors have retold in *A Quetzalcóatl Tale of The Ball Game* is a gentle version of one of many myths surrounding the ball game's origin.

Quetzalcóatl

An Aztec rendering of Quetzalcóatl.

An Aztec rendering of Quetzalcóatl, the feathered serpent, as the god of wind.

Perhaps the earliest incarnation of Quetzalcóatl (ket-zal-CO-atl) was as a sky monster known as the feathered serpent or bird-snake (quetzal = a bird; cóatl = snake). Quetzalcóatl was a major god in Mesoamerican history. He was credited with discovering agriculture, inventing writing, and creating the ball game. He was known by a variety of names. As the god of wind, he was called *Ehecatl*. The Maya called him *Kukulcan*.

Ancient books or manuscripts, called *codices,* were found in the ruins of the Maya and Aztec cultures, and much of the information known about the gods was found there. Quetzalcóatl was described as being tall, robust, and broad of brow. He wore a necklace of seashells and a cloak made of quetzal feathers. He wore anklets of rattles and sandals on his feet. His headdress and belt were serpents. In some pre-Columbian codices, he was shown wearing a mask in his guise as the wind god.

There were many historical or legendary figures over the years who took the name Quetzalcóatl. Priests of the Toltec Indians who lived near what is now Mexico City often took this name. According to one recurring legend in oral history, there was a priest or priest-ruler called Topiltzin-Quetzalcóatl who was a peace-loving and positive leader. In many stories, Quetzalcóatl is fair-skinned and bearded, a story which has intrigued scholars for years and has generated many theories on the origin of the legend.

The human figure of Topiltzin-Quetzalcóatl and the deity Quetzalcóatl often become intertwined in oral tradition. Mesoamerican scholars are still attempting to clarify the actual history of Topiltzin-Quetzalcóatl, the man, and separate it from the myth of Quetzalcóatl, the god.

As with all myths that have been passed down through oral tradition, there are many Quetzalcóatl stories. In some of the different versions of the Quetzalcóatl myths or legends, he is sometimes thought of as a god. Other times, he is portrayed as a man. Sometimes these stories blend together in ways that are hard for us to understand, which is to be expected, as these myths and legends have been retold for thousands of years. Quetzalcóatl was viewed as the embodiment of the goodness of the human soul flying like a bird, as well as the incarnation of the earth in the form of a snake.

The origins of Quetzalcóatl, the deity, are lost in ancient Mesoamerican history. As the legends and tales have filtered down through the ages, they have been reinterpreted by many different storytellers.

Tlaloc

An Aztec rendering of Tlaloc.

The Aztec god of rain was called Tlaloc (TLA-loc). He was also one of the earth gods of fruitfulness. The Maya called him Chac. The Aztecs portrayed Tlaloc with protruding eyes, a twisted nose, and a pleated paper fan at the back of his neck that symbolized fruitfulness and productivity. At times, he was portrayed carrying an ear of corn in one hand and a water flower in the other. Priests sometimes portrayed the rain god in ceremonial services and wore crowns of white Heron plumes to symbolize clouds. In one hand, they carried a shield and in the other they held a staff shaped like lightning. Sometimes the priests' faces were painted blue, or they wore blue masks and their bodies were painted black. Drops of liquid rubber were put on their faces and they wore rubber sandals on their feet. The rubber was to attract the black rain clouds.

In recent times, a huge stone structure of Tlaloc was moved from its original site to its present location in front of the Museum of Anthropology in Mexico City. The move was accompanied by the most torrential downpours that the city had ever experienced. Even more surprising was that this happened during the dry season! Some say the storm was brought on by Tlaloc himself.

Tlaloc (Aztec) with lightning and thunderbolt.

The Quetzal Bird

The quetzal bird is thought to be one of the most beautiful of all birds. It is a member of the trogon family of tropical birds. The quetzal is about the size of a turtledove. The iridescent malachite-green tail feathers of the bird may measure three feet or more in length. The body of the quetzal bird is a shimmering green. The male has a vivid red breast and yellow beak. The female is a smaller version of the male with shorter tail feathers and a black rather than yellow beak. The quetzal bird lives only in high, cool, wet forests. Unfortunately, this beautiful bird is becoming increasingly rare as the rain forests are becoming depleted.

The Aztecs and Maya used the quetzal feathers to adorn the costumes and headdresses of their gods and nobility. The feathers were so important that the Aztecs imposed the death penalty on any commoner who killed a quetzal bird. Quetzalcóatl was portrayed as wearing a headdress or cloak made from quetzal feathers.

Glyphs

Glyphs are a form of picture and word writing found in the ancient codices and on ceremonial buildings found in the Mayan and Aztec ruins. Aztec glyphs were mostly pictures used to identify places and ideas. Mayan glyphs

Mayan glyphs.   **Aztec glyphs.**

were more complex, combining phonics with picture symbols. Color was often added to the glyphs to shade the meanings of the drawings. Details of pre-Columbian life, culture, and history are coming to light as the glyphs are being decoded. Currently, computers are being used to help decipher glyphs as well.

Rubber

Rubber was one of Mesoamerica's major contributions to civilization. Over two hundred kinds of plants produce the milky substance from which rubber can be made. No one tree is the exclusive source of rubber. The commercially grown rubber trees of today probably had very little relationship to the original rubber trees of Mesoamerica.

Hevea brasiliensis (rubber tree).

The people of Mesoamerica discovered they could make resilient, hard balls from the sap of rubber trees. The balls were burned, producing a hot smoky fire. These fires were probably used as incense in certain ceremonies. However, the interesting residue from these ritual fires was a ball with astonishing properties. It had an elasticity that allowed it to almost spring to life when it was thrown. It was this quality in the ball that made it so intriguing.

It took the Europeans several hundred years after Columbus to discover some practical uses for rubber. One of the first uses was to rub out pencil marks—the first eraser. Now, entire industries, commerce, and certainly the world of sports, is indebted to the early discoverers of rubber.

Activities

Vocabulary

Before reading the story, discuss the vocabulary words on pages 30-31 (English) or 32-33 (Spanish). Or, you may choose to introduce new words as you are reading *A Quetzalcóatl Tale of The Ball Game* within the context of the story. For example, read the sentence "Tlaloc kept his maize, gloating all the while." Ask the children what *gloating* might mean. Introduce the remaining vocabulary words in a similar fashion.

As an extension to this activity, have the children pantomime some of the words. Or, ask the children to think of synonyms for each word. Multiple copies of the vocabulary cards can be made and used for concentration games as well.

The words *maize* and *corn* are used interchangeably throughout *A Quetzalcóatl Tale of The Ball Game,* as well as in this teacher's guide. The English word *maize* is derived from *maíz,* the Spanish word for corn. The word *maize* is included in the list of vocabulary words, but you may want to give this word special emphasis because of its importance to the story and the Mesoamerican culture.

Follow-Up Discussion Questions

A list of questions is provided to help guide a class discussion following the reading of *A Quetzalcóatl Tale of The Ball Game* and to encourage critical thinking.

1. Why were Quetzalcóatl and Tlaloc quarreling? How was the ball game a solution to their conflict? Are there better ways to solve differences?

2. What was the ball in the ball game made of? Are balls made of other things? What kinds of things?

3. If you were a spectator at the ball game, which side would you have chosen to cheer for? Why?

4. If you could talk to Tlaloc and Quetzalcóatl, what would you say to each of them?

5. Who was the winner of the ball game? Explain why you think so.

6. How are some current games that we play today similar to the ball game played in ancient Mesoamerica? How are they different?

7. How do you think rubber was made by the pre-Columbian people?

8. What is meant by the words *dicen que* at the beginning of the story?

9. Compare the two gods. Was there a "good guy" and a "bad guy"?

10. If you were a sports commentator, how would you interpret the final outcome of Quetzalcóatl and Tlaloc's game? Who really won?

11. What lesson, if any, is there to be learned from the story of *A Quetzalcóatl Tale of The Ball Game*?

Independent Assignments

The following is a list of activities requiring little or no preparation on the part of the teacher. You might assign certain activities or have students sign up for those they prefer.

1. Draw a picture of what you think is the most important or exciting event that occurred in the story. Write a sentence to go along with the picture.

2. The story reads "Tlaloc kept the maize, gloating all the while." Draw a picture of how someone gloats.

3. Write another ending for the story.

4. Make up a cheer or chant for either side of the ball game.

5. Create a painting of the ball game.

6. Act out the story using puppets or masks.

7. Write a newspaper article for the sports page describing the events of the ball game.

8. Make a diorama of the ball court and the game.

9. Compare the story of the ball game in Mesoamerica with today's Olympic games. Discuss similarities and differences.

Let's Make Tamales!

Traditionally, tamales are served for special festive occasions. Families in Mexico and Central America, as well as families in the United States, sometimes gather together to make tamales. They make as many as they can at one time because preparation of the tamales is so time-consuming. Tamales are made from masa harina (corn flour) dough, stuffed with a meat filling, wrapped in a corn husk, and steam-cooked. Each tamale is rectangular-shaped, about 5" x 2". Making tamales takes a long time, but it's well worth the effort. Because of the time factor for making this food, you may want to divide this activity into a three-day project. The activity may be divided as follows:

Day One: Begin soaking the corn husks. Make the masa dough, cover the dough with a damp cloth, and refrigerate until ready to use.

Day Two: Prepare the meat filling and assemble tamales according to the recipe. Refrigerate until ready to cook.

Day Three: Steam cook the tamales for 45 minutes to an hour. Eat the tamales while they are still warm.

Making tamales is a fun activity for a small group. You will need masa harina (not cornmeal), which is dehydrated masa (corn) flour. Masa harina is sold in bags at most supermarkets or in stores specializing in international foods. Dried corn husks, traditionally used in the making of tamales, can be purchased in food stores in one-pound, prepackaged plastic bags. One pound of corn husks will make about 100 tamales. Use the extra corn husks to make corn husk dolls, if you wish (see page 18).

This recipe calls for a turkey filling, but beef or chicken may be substituted, although these foods were not found in pre-Columbian Mexico. Today, people make a wide variety of tamales. Some tamales are stuffed with pork and seasoned with chili sauce. Seasoned refried beans are sometimes used as a filling, as well as raisins, coconut, nuts, or black olives.

Tamales

(Makes about 25 tamales.)

Preparing Corn Husks

1 corn husk for each tamale, plus several extras

Separate the corn husks. Remove corn silk, clean, and then soak the corn husks in warm water until they are pliable (from 2 hours to overnight). Keep the husks damp until ready to use.

Masa Dough for Tamales

1 1/3 cups (2/3 lb) shortening

4 cups masa harina (dehydrated masa flour)

2 teaspoons salt

2 2/3 cups warm water or meat or poultry broth

Blend all ingredients until the dough holds together well. Cover the dough with a damp cloth and keep it cool until ready to use. This recipe makes 6 cups or enough for about 25 regular-size tamales (each using approximately 3 tablespoons of prepared masa).

Turkey Filling

1 1/2 tablespoons salad oil

1 medium-size onion, chopped

2 cups diced shredded turkey (beef or chicken may be substituted)

2/3 cup mild red chili sauce or mild enchilada sauce

Sauté the onion in hot salad oil until soft. Blend in the turkey and sauce.
Simmer for 10 minutes, stirring occasionally. Cool the mixture for easier handling.

Basic Tamale Procedure

For each tamale, select a prepared, wide, pliable corn husk. Lay the husk flat on a working surface with the tip of the husk away from you. Blot excess water from the corn husk before spreading the masa dough. (If the corn husk is wet, masa will be difficult to spread.) For each tamale, use approximately 3 tablespoons masa dough. Spread the dough on the husk in a rectangular shape, about 5" x 4". The exact size will depend on the length of the corn husk. This rectangle of masa should be placed so that it is completely to the right edge of the corn husk, leaving 2 or 3 inches at the bottom, at least one inch at the left side, and at least 2 inches at the top.

Spoon 1 to 2 tablespoons of meat filling in the center of the masa dough. Fold the right side to the center of the filling. Then fold the left side over the filling, allowing the husk to wrap around the tamale. Fold the bottom end over the mound of dough-enclosed filling and tie it with a strip of thick husk, about 1/4-inch wide. Then fold down the tip of the husk and tie. Place the filled tamales, fold-side down, on a rack above a pot of about six cups of boiling water. Do not allow tamales to touch the water. Cover tightly and steam from 45 minutes to an hour, until the masa is firm. Keep checking the water and add more as needed. Remove and discard husks before eating. Tamales may be frozen in the husk and reheated by steaming them for 20 to 30 minutes.

English/Spanish Vocabulary List of Ingredients for Tamales

shortening	la manteca
salt	la sal
water	el agua
meat	la carne
broth	el caldo
onion	la cebolla
corn husk(s)	la(s) hoja(s) de maíz
cup(s)	la(s) taza(s)
tablespoon(s)	la(s) cucharada(s)
teaspoon(s)	la(s) cucharadita(s)
a can	una lata

Corn Husk Dolls

Materials
corn husks
water
markers or tempera paints
scissors
string

Five or six corn husks are needed to make one corn husk doll. Each husk should be about four or five inches long. Before beginning this activity, soak the corn husks in warm water for approximately five minutes.

Take one husk and roll into a cylinder shape and then fold in half. Tie a piece of husk around the top of the fold, about 3/4" down, to form the head and body. Roll another husk in a cylinder shape and push it through the body part under the neck for the arms. Tie the arms at the end to form hands and to prevent unraveling.

Roll two more husks into cylinder shapes to form legs. Place inside the body husk up to the arms and tie at the waist to prevent the legs from falling out.

To form a dress, take a large husk and cut it in half lengthwise. Place one half with the tip facing up in front of the face and the other half behind the doll's head. Tie both halves at the neck and fold down over the body. Tie the husks at the waist.

To form a shirt, use the same procedure as the dress, except make the husks shorter. Tie the shirt at the waist as well. To form pants, take one husk and cut it in half lengthwise. Wrap one piece around each leg and then tie at the waist. Tie at the bottom of each leg to form feet and prevent unraveling.

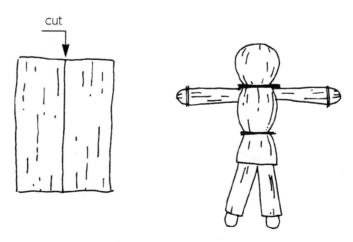

Allow the husks to dry for approximately 30 minutes. Then invite the children to draw faces on their husk dolls using markers or paint. If desired, make a hat by cutting out a circle from an extra husk and then cutting out the center to fit over the top of the head of one of the dolls. A portion of the head should stick out. A shawl can be made by simply draping half of a husk around the doll and pinning the shawl at the neck.

Story Sequencing

Have the children cut out the story sentences provided on the reproducibles on pages 34-36 (English) or 37-39 (Spanish) and then attach each sentence to the bottom of a blank sheet of paper (or half-sheet). Have students create an illustration for each sentence. Children then arrange the pages in sequential order to create a brief book about *A Quetzalcóatl Tale of The Ball Game*.

Play The Ball Game

The students will enjoy playing a game that is very similar to the ball game described in this legend.

Preparations

You will need a large empty room or gymnasium. Tape a cardboard hoop, approximately 7 to 10 inches in diameter, to the center of each wall on either side of the room. You may use two hula hoops, if you wish, to make the game easier.

Hang the hoops perpendicular to the floor, above the students' heads. If it is not convenient to tape the hoops to the walls, you may want to attach the hoops to volleyball poles (see the illustration). For this activity, a large ball (such as a soccer ball or volleyball) should be used, rather than the small ball indicated in the actual story.

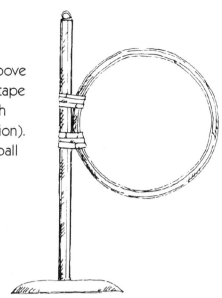

Volleyball pole with hula hoop taped to it.

The Game in Brief

Explain to the children that the game they are going to play is a combination of many different familiar games played with a ball. The rules of this game are that a ball can be passed up and down the court, but no hands or forearms can be used. A team scores a point each time the ball hits the back wall of the opponents' side. If a player is able to get the ball into the air and through the hoop without using his or her hands, that team is the automatic winner of the game, regardless of the score.

Getting Started

Divide the class into two teams. Then choose one player from each team to assume the roles of Quetzalcóatl and Tlaloc. Have Tlaloc and Quetzalcóatl face each other in the center of the court. These two are the primary players of the game, with the rest of the team standing on opposite sides of the court. The teams' role in the game is to stop the ball from going out-of-bounds. Be sure to indicate the boundary lines for the students before beginning the game.

Play Ball!

Toss the ball into the air and have the two primary players use their heads, elbows, knees, feet (not their hands or forearms) to hit the ball. Encourage the rest of the children to deflect the ball in the same way. Throughout the game, choose another player from each team to assume the roles of the gods, alternating the players so that each child gets a chance to play.

Ball Game Pop-Up

Give a copy of the reproducibles on pages 40 and 41 and a file folder to each student. Ask the students to color the ball court background, ballplayers, and hoop using crayons or markers. Encourage the children to create costumes for the players and use a great deal of detail and color. Remind the children to draw protective gear on the players as well, such as gloves, helmets, and so on. The impact of this 3-D display is much more effective if the background and foreground of the file folders are completely colored.

Show the children how to fold the background sheet on the dotted line and cut along the solid lines. Then demonstrate for the children how to tape or glue the background on the inside of a file folder so that the background is on one side and the floor of the ball court is on the other. Cut out each of the players and fold the tabs back. Have the students glue two of the players on the dots provided and the other players on a location of their choice. The ballplayers should stand up at right angles. Glue the hoop to the black dot on the wall of the court. Students may choose to write a description of the ball game to accompany their pop-up.

Making a Rubber-Like Substance

Have children imagine that they have never seen anything with a rubber-like consistency. Have available some "rubber" made from the recipe on page 23, or use Silly Putty (available commercially). Ask the children to pretend they have discovered this substance by accident. What do they think? How can they use it? How will they care for and store their treasure? Ask the children to make up a story of how rubber came to be. While students are working on their stories, call up small groups to make their own "rubber," using the recipe provided.

As an extension to this activity, invite the children to check reference materials for the true story of how rubber was discovered. Why was this substance called *rubber*?

Rubber-Like Substance Recipe

1/4 cup white glue (Elmer's glue)*

2 tablespoons Sta-flo liquid starch

Mix the glue and starch and blend well. Allow the mixture to dry until it is workable. Store in an airtight container. Have children discover as many ways to use their "rubber" as possible. List the different ways on a chart.

*Do not use Elmer's school glue, as it does not bounce or pick up pictures from newsprint. Use the regular brand of Elmer's glue.

Creative Writing or "1-2-3 Surprise!"

A Mayan ballplayer as he appears on the walls of an ancient ball court in the Yucatan.

Invite the children to write a story about two characters who have a conflict. Encourage the students to identify the problem in their stories. Then have the characters solve the problem without fighting. Suggest that children use a sports activity or non-violent show of strength or wit to determine the winner.

Explain to the children that it is often easier to create an interesting story if there is a great imbalance of strength between the two characters. Give students examples, such as a cat and mouse, a bully and smaller child, a wolf and lamb, or an eagle and a robin. Once the children have created a challenge, suggest that they have the more gentle character modify the challenge three times. Remind children that Tlaloc first said he would create a terrible storm to show he was the strongest god. When Quetzalcóatl wouldn't agree, Tlaloc said they would have a war. Still, Quetzalcóatl wouldn't agree. Instead he suggested they play a game with a rubber ball. And, as the children know, that is what the two gods did. Ask the children to describe the "game" of their choice to prove strength and then write a surprise ending.

This activity may work best as a class story with lots of brainstorming along the way. After creating a group story, children may feel more confident about using this story pattern. The "1-2-3 surprise" pattern is used in many familiar fairy tales.

Masks

Masks play an important role in Mesoamerican legends. Explain to the children that priests often wore masks to depict the different gods in their various religious ceremonies. There are many ways you and your class can make masks. Provided here are three sets of instructions for mask-making. Choose the one most appropriate for your students or try all three.

Paper-Bag or Construction-Paper Masks

Materials
paper grocery bag or construction paper
construction-paper scraps
glue
scissors
crayons or markers
glitter, cloth, and other materials that can be glued to paper

Give each child a paper grocery bag or a sheet of construction paper. Provide the children with construction-paper scraps, glue or paste, scissors, crayons or markers, glitter, and other materials to create their own masks. Refer to the story for mask ideas, using pictures of the gods or the colorful Mesoamerican patterns in the glyphs that border the illustrations. Or, the children may have their own ideas about the masks they would like to make. Encourage creativity.

If making masks out of construction paper, cut or punch two small holes on either side of the masks, use gummed reinforcers, and attach string to each hole to tie the masks around the children's heads. Whether using paper bags or construction paper to make the masks, be sure to cut eyeholes in each mask so the children are able to see clearly when wearing them.

Papier-Mâché Masks

Materials
round balloons
newspapers
flour
water
scissors
tempera paint
glue
glitter
cloth or other trimmings

Since this activity uses balloons, it may be more appropriate for older children. Provide a round balloon for each child. After blowing up the balloons, have the children help tear a newspaper into strips. Make a thin paste (approximately the consistency of wallpaper paste) using flour and water. Help the children dip the newspaper strips into the paste and then place the strips over the top half of the balloon. Place at least 4 or 5 layers of newspaper strips over the balloon. Then show the children how to make a small wad from the newspaper and paste the wad to the strips to make a nose.

Let the masks dry completely overnight. When dry, pop the balloons and trim the edges of the masks. With a scissors, help students carefully cut eyeholes in the masks. Then invite the children to paint the masks using tempera paints. Provide glue, cloth, glitter, and other trimmings for the children to use to decorate the masks as they wish.

3-D Masks

Materials
tagboard
pencils
scissors
markers
paper punch
string
feathers or crepe-paper streamers

Duplicate the mask pattern on page 42 (English) or 43 (Spanish) for each child, or make several tagboard mask patterns for the children to trace.

Give each child a 12" x 18" sheet of tagboard. Have children fold the tagboard in half and trace the mask pattern onto each of the folded sides. Make sure the beak edge of the mask is aligned with the fold. Show the children how to cut the mask out through both layers of tagboard. Cut out each eye separately. With an open scissors against a ruler, help the children lightly score the dotted fold lines indicated on the pattern. After the mask is folded, it takes on a three-dimensional form.

Encourage the children to use brightly colored markers to decorate their masks. Children may also use Mesoamerican patterns from the glyphs on the borders of the illustrations in the storybook. Suggest that children use black marker to outline each area of their designs for the most dramatic effect. Discuss design, balance, and symmetry with the children, if you wish.

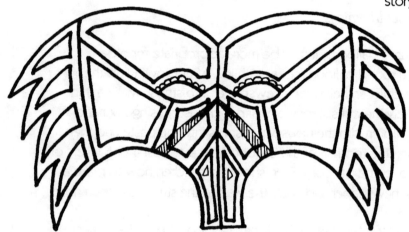

A finished mask.

Gently fold the bottom scored line under the top scored line of the mask. Glue the front edges of the beak together. Now the mask will be three-dimensional. Put a paper-punch hole on each side at the top "feather." Tie a string to each side to tie the mask in place. Attach feathers or crepe-paper streamers to the edges of the mask. Then invite the children to wear their masks in a special parade around the school!

Paper-Bag Puppets

Materials

small paper bags
crayons or markers
scissors
paste or glue

Give each child a copy of the reproducibles on pages 44-47. Provide crayons or markers to color the puppets. Have the children cut out the puppet bodies, heads, and mouth inserts and paste the heads on the bottoms of small paper bags. Paste the mouth insert so it aligns with the head under the bottom flap. Then have the children paste the bodies in place. Invite the children to put on a puppet show with their paper-bag puppets.

Bibliography

Additional Children's Books

Garza, Carmen Lomas. *Family Pictures: Cuadros de Familia,* San Francisco, CA: Children's Book Press, 1990.

Lattimore, D.N. *The Flame of Peace,* New York, NY: Harper & Row, 1987.

Lattimore, D.N. *Why There Is No Arguing in Heaven: A Mayan Myth,* New York, NY: Harper & Row, 1989.

McKissack, Patricia. *The Maya,* Chicago, IL: Childrens Press, 1985.

O'Dell, Scott. *The Feathered Serpent,* Boston, MA: Houghton Mifflin, 1981.

O'Dell, Scott. *The Captive,* Boston, MA: Houghton Mifflin, 1979.

Wisniewski, David. *Rain Player,* New York, NY: Clarion Books, 1991.

Teacher References

Brundage, Burr Cartwright. *The Fifth Sun: Aztec Gods, Aztec World,* Austin, TX: University of Texas Press, 1979.

Brundage, Burr Cartwright. *The Jade Steps: Ritual Life of the Aztecs,* Salt Lake City, UT: University of Utah Press, 1985.

Caso, Alfonso. *The Aztecs: People of the Sun,* Norman, OK: University of Oklahoma Press, 1988.

Coe, Michael D. *Mexico,* New York, NY: Thames and Hudson, 1984.

Gyles, Anna Benson and Sayer, Chlöe. *Of Gods and Men: The Heritage of Ancient Mexico,* New York, NY: Harper & Row, 1980.

Heyden, Doris and Villasenor, Luis Francisco. *The Great Temple and the Aztec Gods,* Claremont, CA: Ocelot Press, 1984.

Johnson, William Weber. *Mexico,* New York, NY: Time, Inc., 1961.

King, Jaime Litvak. *Ancient Mexico: An Overview,* Albuquerque, NM: University of New Mexico Press, 1985.

Nicholson, Irene. *Mexican and Central American Mythology,* New York, NY: Peter Bedrick Books, 1985.

Robicsek, Francis. *Copan, Home of the Mayan Gods,* New York, NY: Museum of the American Indian, Heye Foundation, 1972.

Simpson, B. B. and Conner-Ogorzaly, M. *Economic Botany: Plants in Our World,* New York, NY: McGraw Hill, 1986.

Stephens, John L. *Incidents of Travel in Yucatan,* New York, NY: Dover Publications, Inc., 1963.

Vaillant, George. *Aztecs of Mexico: Origin, Rise, and Fall of the Aztec Nation,* Garden City, NY: Doubleday, 1962.

Von Hagen, V.W. *The Ancient Sun Kingdoms of the Americas: Aztec, Maya, Inca,* Cleveland, OH: World Publishing Co., 1961.

Waters, Frank. *Mexico Mystique: The Coming Sixth World of Consciousness,* Chicago, IL: Sage Books, 1975.

quarrel	gloating
challenge	satisfy
dreadful	spectators

conquered	nobles
precious	maize
tamales	ancestor

discutir	mostrando gran satisfacción (con malicia)
enfrentar	satisfacer
horrible	espectadores

A Teacher's Guide to A Quetzalcóatl Tale of The Ball Game

conquistado(a)	nobles
precioso(a)	maíz
tamales	antepasado

Tlaloc says he will create a terrible storm,
but Quetzalcóatl refuses to let the people
of the earth be harmed.

Tlaloc and Quetzalcóatl stood on the center
circle and faced each other.

Quetzalcóatl and Tlaloc agreed on the rules of the game.

Tlaloc and Quetzalcóatl challenge each other to
see who is the mightiest of all the gods.

A Teacher's Guide to A Quetzalcóatl Tale of The Ball Game © 1992 Fearon Teacher Aids

Quetzalcóatl won the game.

They put on leather gloves and
their heavy deerskin belts.

Tlaloc was happy to grant Quetzalcóatl his wish.

Tlaloc challenges Quetzalcóatl to a war, but Quetzalcóatl
says they can solve their differences without fighting.

The people of the earth are still wondering
who won the best prize.

They built a huge ball court out of stone.

Quetzalcóatl suggests that he and Tlaloc
play a game with a rubber ball.

Tlaloc offers maize as the prize, but Quetzalcóatl
doesn't want Tlaloc's people to go hungry.

Tlaloc dice que va a crear una horrible tormenta, pero Quetzalcóatl no deja que le haga daño a la gente de la tierra.

Tlaloc y Quetzalcóatl estaban de pie y frente a frente en el círculo central.

Quetzalcóatl y Tlaloc acordaron las reglas del juego.

Tlaloc y Quetzalcóatl se desafían uno al otro para ver quién es el más poderoso de todos los dioses.

Quetzalcóatl ganó el juego.

Se pusieron los guantes de piel y sus
cinturones pesados de piel de venado.

Con gusto, Tlaloc le concedió a Quetzalcóatl su deseo.

Tlaloc le dice desafiante a Quetzalcóatl que
tengan una guerra, pero Quetzalcóatl dice que pueden
resolver sus diferencias sin pelear.

La gente de la tierra todavía se pregunta
quién ganaría el mejor premio.

Construyeron una enorme cancha de piedra.

Quetzalcóatl sugiere que él y Tlaloc jueguen
un juego con una pelota de hule.

Tlaloc ofrece maíz como el premio, pero Quetzalcóatl
no quiere que la gente de Tlaloc pase hambre.

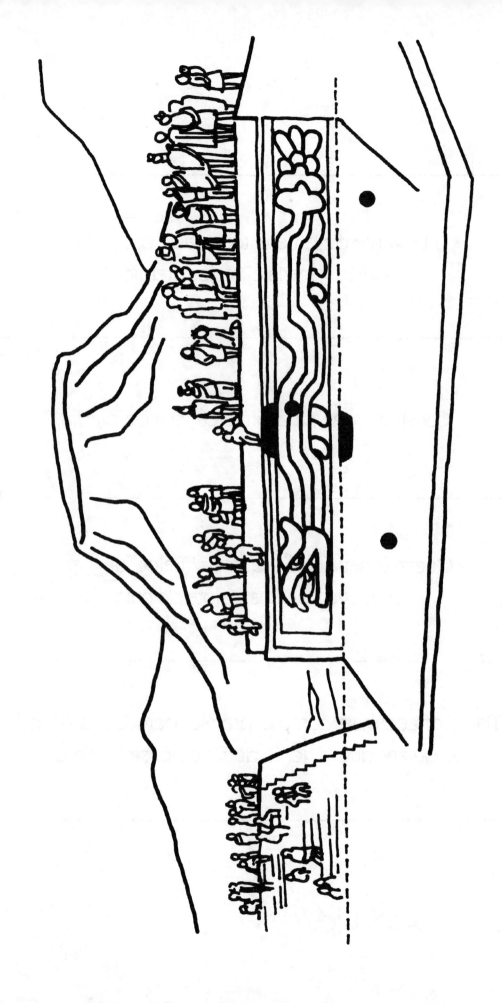

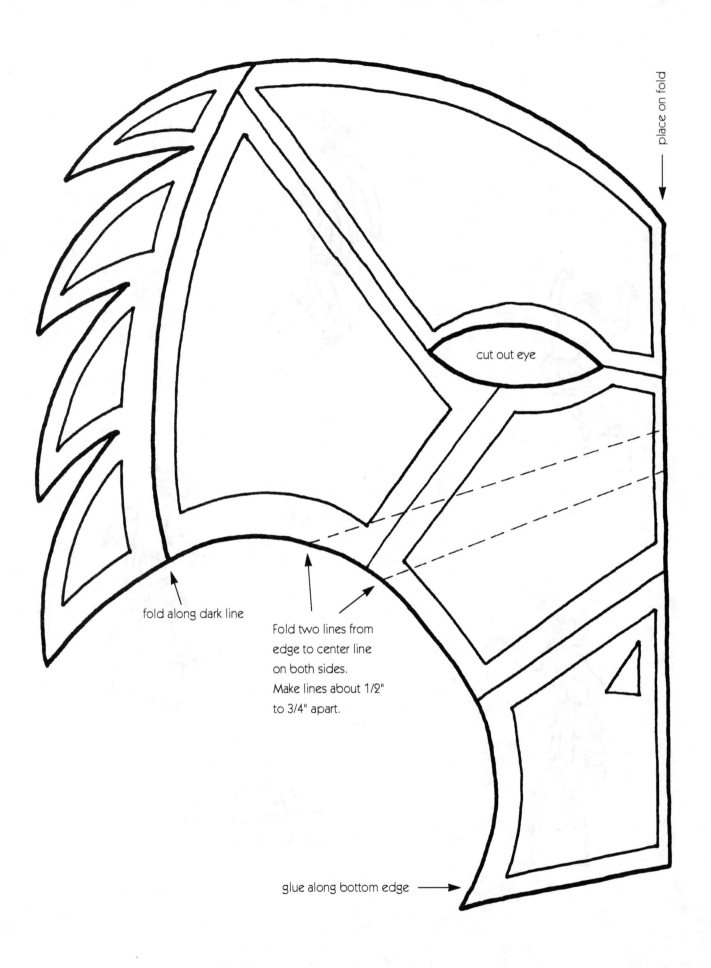

place on fold

cut out eye

fold along dark line

Fold two lines from
edge to center line
on both sides.
Make lines about 1/2"
to 3/4" apart.

glue along bottom edge

A Teacher's Guide to A Quetzalcóatl Tale of The Ball Game © 1992 Fearon Teacher Aids

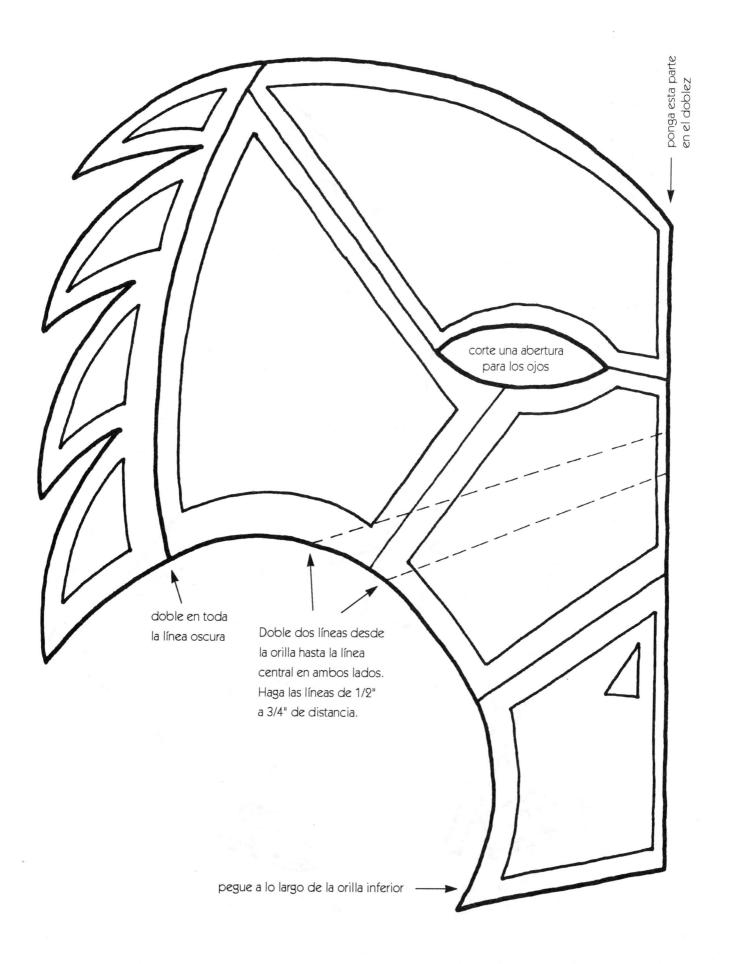

ponga esta parte
en el doblez

corte una abertura
para los ojos

doble en toda
la línea oscura

Doble dos líneas desde
la orilla hasta la línea
central en ambos lados.
Haga las líneas de 1/2"
a 3/4" de distancia.

pegue a lo largo de la orilla inferior

A Teacher's Guide to A Quetzalcóatl Tale of The Ball Game © 1992 Fearon Teacher Aids